Rand Raheem

Handover Strategies in GSM System

GRIN Publishing

Bibliographic information published by the German National Library:

The German National Library lists this publication in the National Bibliography; detailed bibliographic data are available on the Internet at http://dnb.dnb.de .

Imprint:

Copyright © 2011 GRIN Verlag GmbH
Print and binding: Books on Demand GmbH, Norderstedt Germany
ISBN: 978-3-656-27081-2

This book at GRIN:

http://www.grin.com/en/e-book/200825/handover-strategies-in-gsm-system

GRIN - Your knowledge has value

Since its foundation in 1998, GRIN has specialized in publishing academic texts by students, college teachers and other academics as e-book and printed book. The website www.grin.com is an ideal platform for presenting term papers, final papers, scientific essays, dissertations and specialist books.

Visit us on the internet:

http://www.grin.com/

http://www.facebook.com/grincom

http://www.twitter.com/grin_com

**Middlesex
University**

Handover Strategies in GSM System

A Dissertation submitted to Middlesex University as a
requirement for Master of Science degree in
Telecommunications Engineering

By

Rand Hussein Raheem

October 2011

School of Engineering and Information Sciences Hendon

NW4 4BT

United Kingdom

Abstract

GSM is one of the greatest wireless technologies in the world because of the benefits it provides to its users in saving time and its ability in speeding signals. Unfortunately, under the GSM system, the signal interference which users might experience when moving from one coverage area to another presents a real problem. The main objective of this project was to investigate and simultaneously resolve the problem of the GSM handover system. This project is explaining the mechanism of the signal transmits and handover from one antenna to another taken into consideration that transmission may vary according to the type of the handover.

The project attempted then to introduce and compare between all these different types of handover, and decide the ideal type for reserving the signal from any cut or interference. The location of the MS is really the core in tackling the signal interference problem under the system. Therefore, the optimal timing and distance between handover facilities was calculated to solve the problem. The focus of this project is on vertical handover and specially the time before vertical handover. Later on, the project also showed the calculations concerning timing and distance between antennas (or coverage areas) by taking into account the velocity of the mobile node movement. In short, the focus of this project is to investigate the GSM signal interference problem, find the solutions to these problems through the calculation of the ideal timing and distance between antennas and then apply these calculated results in constructing GSM handover facilities.

This project is attempting to provide GSM users with the smoothest and the most secure signal connection when travelling between coverage areas. Matlab program will be used in order to calculate both time and distance of vertical handover. All the results were listed to prove the manual calculations. A conclusion ended the project summing up the main findings of the study and some suggestions for further studies were offered.

It is to be mentioned here that the previous works specifically the one that is concerning about calculating the time and distance of TBVH were the foundation of this project. Unlike other researches who used the OPEN modeller, this project is using Matlab software to calculate the time and distance of TBVH. As a matter of fact, the present study gave a pseudo code in Matlab for predicting the position of vertical handover. It is important to notify that this thesis has considered HO types, issues, solutions, effects, differences and designing Matlab program etc.

Table of Contents

List of figures

List of tables

Abbreviations

1. **HO:** Handover (in British language) or Handoff (in American language)
2. **GSM:** old name (Groupe Special Mobile), new one (Global System for Mobile communications)
3. **Matlab:** matrix laboratory
4. **WLAN:** Wireless Local Area Network
5. **SMS:** Short Message Service
6. **SIM:** Subscriber Identity Module
7. **GPRS:** General Packet Radio Services
8. **ESS:** Extended Service Set
9. **SSID:** Service Set ID
10. **EDGE:** Enhanced Data Rate for GSM Evolution
11. **AMPS:** Advanced Mobile Phone System
12. **TACS:** Total Access Communications
13. **NMT:** Nordic Mobile Telephone system
14. **ISDN:** Integrated Services Digital Network
15. **TDM:** Time Division Multiplexing
16. **MS:** Mobile Station
17. **MSL:** Mobile Station Location
18. **BTS:** Base station Transceiver Station
19. **BSC:** Base station Controller
20. **EIR:** Equipment Identity Register
21. **MSC:** Mobile Switching Centre
22. **HLR:** Home Location Register
23. **GSMSC:** Gateway Mobile Switching Centre
24. **IWMSC:** Interworking Mobile Switching Centre
25. **AUC:** Authentication Centre
26. **GCR:** Group Call Register
27. **SIWF:** Shared Interworking Function
28. **IWF:** Interworking Function
29. **VLR:** Visitor Location Register
30. **IMSI:** International Mobile Subscriber Identity

31. **SACCH:** Slow Access Control Channel

32. **FACCH:** Fast Access Control Channel

33. **BSSMAP:** Base Station Subsystem Mobile Application Part

34. **FDMA:** Frequency Division Multiplexing Access

35. **TDMA:** Time Division Multiplexing Access

36. **CDMA:** Code Division Multiplexing Access

37. **VOIP:** Voice over Internet protocol

38. **ITU:** International Telecommunication Union

39. **MSCTP:** Mobile Stream Control Transmission Protocol

40. **MTSO:** Mobile Telephone Switching Office

41. **RSS:** Received Signal Strength

42. **NCOH:** Network Controlled Handoff

43. **MAHO:** Mobile Assisted Handoff

44. **DECT:** Digital Enhanced Cordless Telecommunications or Digital European Cordless Telephone

45. **QoS:** Quality of Services

46. **MT:** Mobile Terminal

47. **TBVH:** Time Before Vertical Handover

48. **AP:** Access Point

49. **MN:** Mobile Node

50. **TD:** Time Division

51. **SPPQ:** Signal Prediction Priority Queuing

52. **CBS:** Current Base Station

53. **NXBS:** next Base station

54. **ETSI:** European Telecommunication Standards Institute

55. **TG:** Telecommunication Group

56. **IP address:** Internet Protocol address

57. **VHO:** Vertical Handover

Acknowledgment

I would like to thank the almighty Allah most graceful, most compassionate for the strength He has given me to pursue this task and stand firm in the face of challenges and there were so many. Thanks are to Him for the opportunity He has blessed me and enabled to do my MSC in Telecommunication Engineering, and for the faith He has implanted in my heart and soul.

This dissertation has been written with the support and assistance of a number of people, I would like to personally thank. At my university, I owe my deepest gratitude to my supervisor, Dr. Aboubaker Lasebae, whose expertise, understanding and patience added considerably to my graduate experience.

Moreover, I would like to thank the other members of my committee for the knowledge and the huge amount of information that I gained from their lectures and seminars, Dr. Leonardo Mostarda, Dr. Shahedur Rahman, Dr. Purav Shah and Mr. Ihab Arusi.

Finally, I would like to thank my family for the support they provided me with through my entire life and through my dissertation because without their love, encouragement and financial support and moral assistance, I would not have finished this course.

Chapter 1

GSM HO overview and scanning concept through WLAN

1. Introduction

The mobile telephone has become an indispensable part of human life because it endows it with mobility and availability. The continuous development in the field of GSM technology connects mobile telephone to networks. The functionality to ensure an acceptable quality of a mobile call when moving from one coverage area to another is called Handover. As a matter of fact, Handover is a process used when the quality of the signal decreases as a result of moving from one coverage area to another. Handover technique transfers the signal of the call transparently from one stationary antenna to another during the call to maintain the signal and to avoid any cut that might happen because of the weakness in both signal and power. There are different types of GSM handover, each one of these types has its own properties which make it unique and different from others. Handover has its own advantages and disadvantages (problems) which are under both investigation and development. In this project, there will be an explanation of the mechanism of the signal transmission and handover from one antenna to another. Moreover, a comparison of the different types of handovers will be made in order to select the best type that can reserve the signal from any cut or interference. Moreover, to resolve the problems and the obstacles that might face the transmitted signal from any cut or interference, this project will calculate the optimal timing and distance for vertical handover between handover facilities to render a solution that can solve these problems.

As an introduction for this project, it will be necessary to understand few concepts which give a general overview before starting the focus of this paper such as:

1. History of GSM.
2. Overview of GSM handover.
3. The connection establishment in WLAN and the scanning concept.

1.1 History of GSM

Nowadays, GSM cell or mobile phone system has become more popular than any other system because of the widely usage in both the local and global levels. GSM is a system which is rich with several features and applications such as: SMS text messages, SIM cards, international roaming and internet. The internet applications have been improved dramatically since new technologies have been introduced such as GPRS and EDGE.

The first cell phone system was developed in 1989. Actually, it was an analogue system. Typically, the old system used the frequency modulated carriers for the voice channel and the data carried on a separate shared control channel. A report from Radio-Electronics.com [25] states that two major systems existed at that time; those were the AMPS that was used in USA and TACS that was used in UK. Moreover, another system was developed called NMT. In fact, it was the first commercial system to be developed in the area of cellular systems; the significant financial benefits were the motivating factor behind the maximization of the GSM system.

In 1982, the basic criteria of the new cellular system were listed to meet the user needs; these criteria included the good voice quality, low cost, international roaming, the ability to support handheld terminals, new services and facilities, efficient spectral, large capacity and ISDN compatibility. The technological developments and related experiments that took place at that time evinced that TDM offered a good performance with the new technology than other techniques did.

In 1991, the GSM system saw its first dawning. It was indeed a farfetched target to investors; however the real beginning was in 1992. By the end of 1993, the GSM had attracted more than one million subscribers; the number was increasing rapidly and constantly. Nowadays the number is being increasing and it has indeed exceeded three billion subscribers.

Because of the wide usage of the GSM in many world countries, it was crucially necessary to change its name from Group Special Mobile to a Global System for Mobile communications.

1.2 Overview of GSM handover

To begin with, it is quite necessary to mention the basic entities of the GSM system as depicted in the following figure:

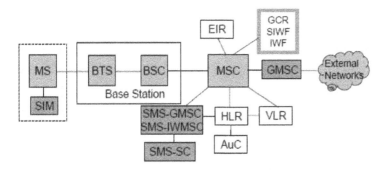

Fig (1): The reference model of GSM [1]

The random movement of the mobile node from the coverage area of one cell to another has made it necessary to find a new mechanism by which calls can be transferred from one cell to another without cutting off the call. A report from phonehistory.co.uk [21] proposed that there are two situations for this mechanism to function; these situations are between calls and during calls.

1.2.1 Between calls

In the idle mode, the mobile reports only when it transfers to another VLR by doing a location update. Since each mobile has to report its new position by sending a position update, the network might mislay some of these calls as a result of the huge database or a signalling error. Therefore, to avoid this problem it is better for the mobile to avoid sending more than one report at the same time. In this way, the user might receive an old SMS message or being told to wait for a long voicemail when the process of location update is taking place. When the mobile phone is closed, it sends a log-off signals to the network so that it will not look for a switched off mobile known as an IMSI Detach. It is impossible to avoid such situation specially when the switched off mobile is out of the coverage area. So in this situation the network will not take notice the switched off mobile until the next scheduled location update has been missed.

13

1.2.2 During a call

As long as the call is in progress and during the time between sending and receiving data, the handset has the responsibility of monitoring the signal it gets from the 16 nearby cells and are listed in the currents neighbour list of the required cell. Every second, it reports the level signal of one of the best six neighbouring cells to the BSC by using SACCH. The decision of switching cells can vary but in general the process accrues to the cell that has the best signal and this subsequently economises the power in the mobile. The organization and coordination of the handover process is a time-critical function; therefore, it is necessary to use FACCH.

Moreover, the decision can be made either by the mobile itself or the BTS but since the BTS sometimes might be too busy, the handover fails and the mobile needs to start scanning again the network for a fresh start. This can occur because of the signal propagation over far distances over hilltops or mountains where no neighbouring listed cells exist near the mobile.

1.3 The connection establishment in WLAN and the scanning concept

Bing (2008) [3] states in his book that because of the absence of a stable physical network connection in WLANs, the MN spends more time and resources in order to scan the surrounding area and to look for optimum wireless coverage. Even when the MN is connected to an AP, the mobile does not guarantee the connectivity within the required period of time due to the mobility and the fluctuation in the channel conditions. In this case, it might be necessary to migrate the mobile data to another AP in order to avoid any connection loss.

It is to be mentioned here that the main aim of wireless devices is not only looking for APs, but also offering the best optimum connectivity .The establishment of this connectivity can be described in the following figure:

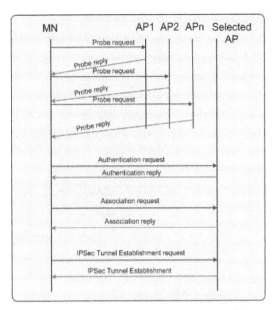

Fig (2): The connection establishment in WLAN [3]

The connection establishment in WLAN processes through the following FOUR steps:

1.3.1 Discovery

To establish a connection between the MN and the AP, the wireless device scans all the radio channels in the surrounding area to detect the AP and other stations. However, this scanning might be either passive or active. In the passive case, the MN listens to the radio channels for beacon transmitted by the APs and after that decides the best choice. However, in the active scan, the MN sends an explicit probe request for each AP having the ability to transmit beacons in response.

1.3.2 Authentication

This can be achieved through exchanging special authenticate packets. The association request starts its progress only when authentication is verified. Otherwise, the recipient sends a de-authentication notifying the requested device.

1.3.3   Association, Disassociation and Re-association

This step seeks to establish an association between the stations or between the station and the AP. When the MN intends to connect to an AP in a BSS, it sends an association request. When handing occurs between the old AP and the new one, the MN sends the disassociation request to the old AP and a re-association to the new AP. Each MN has the ability to connect only with one AP at a particular time. It also consists of the mechanisms responsible for the QoS and the call admission control.

1.3.4   Confidentiality

This is a necessary step to ensure the encrypted form of communication between the two devices that share the public wireless interface. The AP in the BSS has the full responsibility of enforcing the security policies and to advertise these policies in beacon and probe response packets.

1.3.5   The AP discovery and association

In WLAN MN, deciding the AP implies scanning for the availability of different APs before making the final choice of the most appropriate AP. According to Bing (2008) [3], scanning can be initiated in two ways; manually by the subscriber or automatically by the deployment of system selection algorithm. The above mentioned types of scanning namely the passive and the active will be explained in details in the following subsections.

1.3.5.1 Passive scanning

Bing (2008) [3] states that in passive scanning, joining a particular ESS, the MN requires listening to different channels consecutively searching for beacon frames which match the service ID (SSID) of the ESS. However, passive scanning is more time consuming than active scanning.

1.3.5.2 Active scanning

In the active scanning, the MN requests for a beacon frame of each channel through the transmission of the probe requested packets. After that, the MN listens to the channel for a beacon from the AP e.g. 200ms and then it moves to scan another channel as soon as it receives a reply. Finally, the MN creates a list of the available APs at the end of the scanning procedure.

However, Ghini, Ferretti and Panzieri (2010) [12] state in the IEEE that some criteria should be taken into account to select an AP for attachment .This criteria is shown in the following:

   i.   The AP with the highest and strongest filtered value e.g. 75dBm will be selected.

   ii.   The AP with long duration of time will be selected too.

   iii.   A combination of the two above criteria is also accepted.

2. Literature review

The main purpose of this part is to present an overview of some related works.

2.1 Definition of the handover process

UMTS.com (2011) [36] defines the handover or handoff as the process of transferring the user connection from one radio channel to another while moving from one coverage area to another .The purpose is to maintain the call connection and avoids the call dropping. In another word, Ramsdale, Walden and Gaskell (1994) [28] say that handover is a technique which allows calls to be maintained while the mobile moves from one coverage area to another; otherwise the call will be dropped. The following figure clarifies this process of handover:

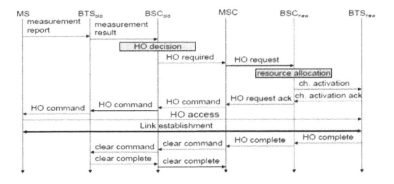

Fig (3): handover procedure [28]

17

2.2 Types of Handover technique

A report from Radio-Electronics.com (2011) [24] shows that there are four types of GSM handover which can be verified according to their locations, slots, frequencies, mobile nodes movement and the coverage areas:

- **Intra-BTS handover**: Here interference or noise changes the frequency or the slot of the GSM .In spite of this change, the mobile maintains connection with the same base station transceiver.

- **Inter-BTS Intra BSC handover**: This type of handover occurs when the mobile gets out of the coverage area controlled by the same BSC.

- **Inter-BSC handover**: MSC is responsible for controlling this type of handover. When the mobile goes out of the range of controlled cells by BSC, a handover process is needed to be maintained over either the BTC or the BSC.

- **Inter-MSC handover**: This type of handover takes place when there is a change in the network. The two MSCs control the handover technique.

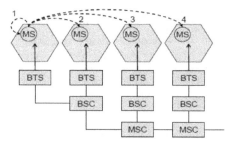

Fig (4): Types of handover [24]

18

2.3 Reasons of Handover Failure

A report by Gnnettest.com (2011) [14] , identifies the reasons behind the handover failure. They can be summarized as:

- **Radio interface failure:** This problem is caused by interference, wrong cell parameters, BTS hardware problems, antenna problems, etc.
- **No radio resource available:** which means there is no radio channel available in a particular cell for the new user to make connect with.
- **Invalid cell:** this problem happens when there is a certain cell that undefined in the MSC database.
- **Invalid message contents:** This is related to a signalling error or having an error with the signal once it is transmitted.
- **Equipment failure:** This is considered to be the most common failure. It happens when the equipment does not follow the regular procedures identified in the BSSMAP protocol that describes how the messages are being transferred between the BSS and the MSC (ETSI.com, 2011) [10] . Moreover, this failure might occur when the system engineers do not follow the ETSI, which governs the telecommunication mechanisms (Protocols.com, 2011) [23].
- **Number of HOs:** This problem is due to the complexity of HO protocol. And as a result, the GSM system avoids the unnecessary handoffs. Moreover, because of the random numbers of shadow fading, HO points can be disrupted around the best point and that might cause a large number of handoffs (Dr. Pesch, 2000) [20].

A report from Thomsen and Manggaard, (2003) [33] furnishes more information about the failures in GSM handover:

- **Call lost**

The call can be lost before or during the handover process due to the decrease of the quality level of the radio link. In this case; the GSM network does not have a big chance to fix this situation. Therefore, it is necessary to release all allocated resources. The call can be lost after the resources of the new BSS are allocated or before of the switching off the call. However, in this case the resources should be deallocated in both new and old BSS because if the call is ended by one party during the handover, the same resource deallocation should take the place of the other party.

- **MS fails to access the new BSS**

When sending a HND_CMD to the MS, the MS accesses the new BSS. However, the MS does not synchronize the new BSS. This synchronization might fail once the MS goes back to the old BSS and indicates the failure.

- **Incompatible equipment**

The new BS should have the same features of the old BS to save the call. For example, if the new BS does not support using ciphering algorithm, it will not be able to save the call. The new BSS signals the failure to the MS.

2.4 The differences between hard, soft and softer handovers

Handover technique can be classified into three categories: hard handover, soft handover and softer handover (UMTS.com, 2011) [35]. Moreover, those categories can be explained as follow:

- **Hard handover**

  Hard handover or (break before make) occurs when the old radio link breaks the connection with the old BS the mobile moves out of the coverage area before the new link is established with the new BS. There are two types of hard handover: seamless hard handover and non-seamless hard handover. With seamless hard handover, the user cannot recognise it while user can recognise the non-seamless hard handover. However, Bhatia and Stevetuf (2008) [2] say that hard handover requires changes in frequency carriers and that it is easier to be implemented and cheaper than soft handover. Hard handover can be used with FDMA or TDMA because these access systems can reduce the interference of different frequency ranges. It is to be mentioned here that hard handoff technique is appropriate as delay in traffic is allowable. Most designed applications, such as technology-enabled internet, VOIP, and WiMax, work with more precision when that technique is used. The following figure explains this:

20

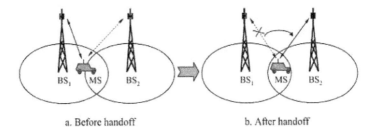

a. Before handoff   b. After handoff

Fig (5): Hard handover [13]

- **Soft handover**

Bhatia and Stevetuf (2008) [2] points out that soft handover (or make before break) is a mechanism happens when the mobile moves out of the coverage area. It establishes connection with the new BS before disconnecting link with the old BS. Moreover, soft handover is more reliable in network access with less time delay in comparison with the hard handover. This process enables several frequency channels to function simultaneously minimizing fading or interference within those frequencies. Furthermore, soft handover is suitable for voice networks, such as CDMA or GSM and for high critical communication media like videoconferencing. The following figure explains this:

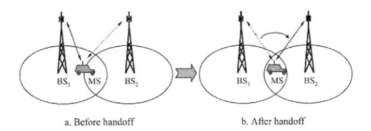

a. Before handoff   b. After handoff

Fig (6): Soft handover [13]

- **Softer handover**

In his presentation, Khan (2010) [16] states that softer handover is a private case of soft handover which takes place when the radio link is added and removed inside the same node. For example, softer handover happens between two sectors of two overlapping cells as depicted in Figure (7):

21

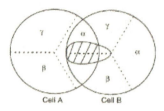

Fig (7): Softer handover [22]

2.5 SYNC handovers and asynchronous handover

Duval (2006) [6] states in his article that the handover mechanise consists of the synchronous (concurrency) mode and the asynchronous (not-concurrency) mode. In the synchronous mode, the destination cell and the origin cell are synchronised by measuring the difference in the time slots respectively. The mobile itself can calculate the consuming time in advance. And this enables the new channel to tune the transmission and thus speeds up the handover. On the other hand, asynchronous mode means that both of the destination cell and the origin cell are not synchronised. In order to calculate the timing advance, it is necessary to identify the MT and the new BTS. After that, the mobile terminal sends a sequence of access flows by setting the time advance on zero through several messages. Then, the BTS calculates the necessary timing advance by using a round-trip time delay of the messages. In other words, Rajkamalvashistha (2011) [26] summarises, in his article, the synchronous and the asynchronous modes. He says that when two cells are connected with the same TG of the same TG cluster, they form a synchronized cell. In other words, they are synchronized by the timing function of the same TG. On the other hand, the asynchronous mode occurs when there are two cells belonging to two different TG.

2.6 Emergency handovers

According to Umair (2009) [34], emergency handover takes place when the mobile moves from one cell to another. The frequency of one BTS goes up and down dramatically and this in turn might cause a call drop problem. Therefore, the BSC will check the necessity of the handover by determining the channel quality and the signal strength of both the current cell and the adjacent cell.

2.7 Vertical and Horizontal handovers

According to Latif and khan (2009) [17] , handoff consists of the following two techniques:

- **Horizontal Handover**
  This technique occurs when the user implements the same network access and mobility performed on the same layer. Shaikh (2010) [29] states that this type of handoff happens when a mobile node moves from one BS to another belonging to the same level of the network hierarchy. Moreover, it can be referred to as an intra-handover. The ITU (2008) [15] states that, the main target of horizontal handoff is maintaining on-going service regardless of any change in the IP address. To maintain on-going service, it is necessary to hide the changed IP address for example the mobile IP or the dynamically updating of the changed IP address (MSCTP). The majority of handover mechanism might include the horizontal handoff and that due to the ability of maintaining the on-going service regardless of any IP address changes.

- **Vertical Handover**
  This technique happens when the user moves among different networks and their different layers. Shaikh (2010) [29] points out that vertical handover happens when the mobile node switches its connection to a new network BS that might be higher or lower than the current network. It is to be mentioned here that vertical handoff can be referred to as Inter handoff. In this regard, ITU (2008) [15] states that vertical handover occurs when the user moves across heterogeneous access networks completely different from the horizontal handover. The access technology and the IP address are changeable due to the movement of the in-between mobile node. Therefore, the vertical handover service goes on regardless of changes in the IP address or the network interference. This part will be discussed in details because it is the focus of the project.

The following tables are a comparison of both the horizontal handoff and the vertical handoff:

Table 1:

Differences between vertical and horizontal handovers [17]

	Vertical Handover	Horizontal Handover
Access Technology	Changed	Not changed
QoS Parameters	May be hanged	Not changed
IP Address	Changed	Changed
Network Interface	May be change	Not Changed
Network Connection	More than on connections	Single connection.

Table 2:

Differences in the capability of horizontal and vertical handovers [15]

	Horizontal handover	Vertical handover
Access technology	Single technology	Heterogeneous technology
Network interface	Single interface	Multiple interface
Actually used IP address at a time	Single IP address	Multiple IP address
QoS parameter	Single value	Multiple values
Network connection	Single connection	Multiple connections

The following figure shows the difference between vertical and horizontal handovers in wireless network:

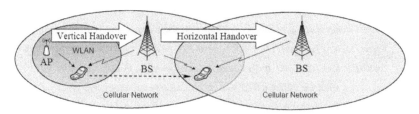

Fig (8): Example of vertical and horizontal [40]

2.8 "Multilayer Handover" Strategy, "Ping pong effect" and "take-back"

Ekiz (2006) [8] states that multilayer handover has been designed to decrease the number of handovers and increase the capacity of the system. In multilayer handover, the number of microcells are added and controlled by the macro cell that gives users the ability to assign each layer according to its speed. The microcells and the macro cells have the capability to cover area ranges between 500 meters and 35 km. The number of handovers requests decreases because the number of slow users is assigned to the microcells whereas the number of fast users is assigned to the macro cells. However, macro cells have the ability to serve the slow users when microcells are overloaded and congested. According to Ramsdale and Harrold (1992) [27], the selection of the fast and slow users is determined by a switching parameter and a cell selection penalty.

On the other hand, Wowra (2011) [38] discusses the effect of ping pong which occurs in cities or mountainous regions that might block the line of the signal and thus causes unnecessary handovers between neighbouring cells especially when a stronger signal is received from a neighbouring cell. Theses unnecessary handovers should be decreased through the handover decision making stage. However, Shaikh (2010) [29] defined this effect as undesirable effect which happens when the mobile node does many unnecessary handovers between two BSs as a result of the fluctuations in the channel resources which in turn cause over loadings or even losing the signal.

However, Ekiz (2006) [8] believes that another case can be derived from the multilayer handover while the microcell is allocating its own channels; the new handover calls overflow to the macro cell layer. The take back process takes place when the load of the micro cell decreases.

2.9 Handover decisions in GSM

Ekiz, Salih, Küçüköner and Fidanboylu (2010) [9] discuss handover making decision protocol by using different cellular systems as shown below:

> **Network Controlled Handover (NCHO)**

Network Controlled Handover has been used in the first generation cellular systems, like the AMPS where the MTSO took the handover decision. In Network Controlled Handover, the network is responsible of both the RSS measurements and the handover decision. The handover causes high time delay when the network is overloaded.

> **Mobile Assisted Handover (MAOH)**

In NCOH, the load of the network is high because the network itself has the full responsibility of the handover process; to reduce this load; the MS performs the RSS measurements and sends them respectively within a periodic time to the BS in the MAHO. Eventually the MSC decides when to handoff.

> **Mobile Controlled Handover (MCOH)**

MCOH assigns the responsibility of making handover decision and control to the MS. The MS and the BS make the needed measurements and the BS sends it to the MS. Then the MS decides when to handoff. The application of the MCOH is the DECT which is a simple cellular system with 100-500 ms handover execution time.

2.10 GSM handover solutions

A survey from Akki and Chadchan (2008) [1] points out some issues the GSM Handover faces. They are as follow:

- **QoS:** The main factor behind this problem is handover blocking due to limited resources, cell losses, out-of-order cell delivery, delay and delay variations. Minimizing them might cause a disruption in the cost of buffering. It is worth mentioning here that QoS is responsible of timing and synchronization issues.

- **Rerouting Connection:** The new algorithms to find new route options and establish signalling protocols to refigure the connection path are still developing

- **Point to Multipoint.** Here again, the process of developing protocols that can reroute the point to multipoint connections of MTs has not been finalized yet.

- **Mobile-to-Mobile Handoff:** This mechanism is still needed to address the up gradation of existing protocols in order to support the connection routing and the QoS for a mobile to mobile connection.

- **Optimization:** one of the challenges that face HO technique is developing an efficient method that allows an existing MT connection to be periodically rerouted along the optimal path.

2.11 Mathematical calculations and modulations

The mathematical calculations and modulations based handover prediction consists of many theories predicting the future of handover by applying mathematical formulas and models. Therefore, it is necessary to develop an efficient solution based on the available information about the MN movement.

Ebersman and Tongus (1999) [7] emphasise the importance of knowing the time of the mobile node before having a handover. They propose the SPPQ method that calculates the expected time of the MN before reaching the boundary of the cell and performing the horizontal handoff based on the RRS. However, this study fails to capture the accuracy of the mobile node movement from one point to another and it is incomplete.

Furthermore, Shen, Mark and Ye (2000) [31] proposed in their paper an adaptive system predicting the probability in which the MN would be able to enter a particular cell in a particular time (t). This approach takes into account the current and previous power signal measurements in to predicate the future mobility information. All the BS power signal measurements which are received at the MN are sent to the MSC

27

through the home BS which has the ability to perform the prediction calculations. This proposed solution takes into account realistic measurements in order to predict the next cell in which the MN is expected to handoff. However, this study is limited to that function only and does not predict the time in which the MN is likely to remain in the coverage area of the current cell. Also, it demonstrates acceptable performance in homogeneous networks when the BS count is less than six, because after that computational overhead increases significantly. And this in turn might cause problems in the heterogeneous networks when a MN may sense different BSs from different networks at any given instant.

Moreover, Makela (2000) [4] proposed a predictive handover approach employed on the MN movement as a way to predict the position of the MN and the distance to the cell border. But the problem with this proposal is that it does not calculate the sudden changes and movements of the mobile node.

Another study carried out by Duong (2004) [5] proposed an estimation for the shortest waiting time of transmitting the MN information to the new access network. However, this study is only focuses on the concept of forced handover during the actual switching of network interference without focusing on the concept of applying this study to achieve an improved vertical handover prediction.

Moreover, there are two popular methods to calculate the distance between the MN and the AP; the RSS-based and the Co-ordinate based. In a recent study, Xiaohuan (2008) [39] [40] adopts the RSS based distance method which calculates the AP-MN distance from path loss models as the following equation shows:

$$RSS_P = E_t - 10\beta log_{10}l_{OP} + \varepsilon \quad \text{[32]}$$

However, the above method suffers from two drawbacks; firstly, while it might be possible to calculate the AP-MN distance, the required information itself might not be enough to locate the MN. Secondly, the accuracy of the RSS-based method depends mostly on the RSS measurements which might be poor due to the RSS fluctuation. The above problem is visible mostly in Xiaohuan (2008) [39] [40] study where the distance estimation error increases up to 70% due to the increase in the RSS samples when the MN's velocity decreases below 10 m/s.

Therefore, it is necessary to propose mathematical calculations and implement a mathematical program to calculate the time before vertical handover and the distance to choose the best time and the perfect distance for performing this process as shown below.

3. The focus - Calculate the optimal timing and distance for GSM vertical handover between two antennas

The main purpose of this chapter is to calculate the time and the perfect location of handover in order to reduce the issues of unnecessary handovers, lost calls, time delays and noise in the signal. Shaikh (2010) [29] proposed in her paper that the problem of unnecessary handover is due to the difficulty in recognising the temporary coverage, the limitation in the required resources and the congestion that might be in the new network.

It is important at the beginning to mention why vertical handover has been chosen instead of the other types of handover. As mentioned above, vertical handover takes place when the mobile node switches its connection to a new BS with different access technology. This new access technology might be higher or lower than the current network in the hierarchy system. Shaikh (2010) [29] explains that in the case of the upward vertical handover, the mobile node switches from a small coverage area with high bandwidth to a large coverage area with low bandwidth e.g. from WLAN to UMTS. On the other hand, the downward vertical handover is completely the opposite of the upward vertical handover.

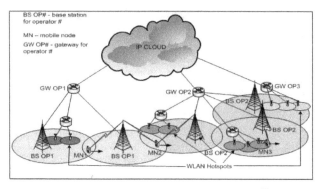

Fig (9): The scenarios of handover in 4G networks [29]

3.1 Time Before Vertical Handover (TBVH)

In this section, the process of mathematical calculations of the TBVH will be presented. Three important parameters will be the focus of the suggested model of TBVH. These three parameters are; the distance between MN and AP, MN velocity and MN direction of motion. The targets of the mathematical calculations focus on both; the indoor and the outdoor environments. The new technique of TBVH is derived from the available information, the distance from the BS, the velocity of the MN and the direction of the MN.

Some importation features of the network topology should be available to calculate TBVH accurately. For example, some topology changes might happen in the BSs at network boundaries known as BBS. The BBS has the responsibility of informing the MN about the possible network environments: outdoor and indoor. In the outdoor environment, the BBS informs the mobile node about the vertical handover threshold .Whereas in the indoor environment, it tells the dimensions of the enclosed space of the position of the various exits. Moreover, the BBS can inform the MNs about other networks in the surrounding area which might have undiscovered vertical handover to make.

3.1.1 Time Before Vertical Handover (for outdoor environments)

This scenario is concerned with the mobile node in an outdoor setting but under the WLAN coverage, moving in the direction of the BS boundary with a velocity v as the following figure shows:

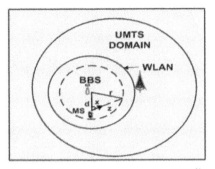

Fig (10): MN under the coverage of the BBS [30]

The considered networks are UMTS (or GSM) and WLAN where any other networks can be used. Here, a circular coverage cell has been suggested with a radius R instead of the hexogen cell. The above figure shows the inner dotted circle with a radius r; both represent the handover threshold when the mobile node is expected to have a vertical handover. Moreover, x is the angle made by the MN when moving towards the BBS. D is the distance between the MN and the BBS. Z is the point on the threshold circle when the MN expects to have a vertical handover. Applying Pythagoras theorem, the following equation will be used to calculate z

$$r^2 = d^2 + z^2 \qquad \text{So, } z^2 = r^2 - d^2$$

But here, the direction of the mobile movement is necessary, the equation will be:

$$r^2 = d^2 + z^2 - 2dz\cos x$$

However, due to some mathematical and geometric considerations, a one root of the quadratic equation will be taken as the following equation shows:

$$z = (d \cos x) + \sqrt{r^2 - d^2 \sin^2 x}$$

As a matter of fact, the formula of velocity is the distance over time, so time is the distance over velocity. Then, TBVH can be calculated by the following equation:

$$TBVH = \frac{(d\cos x) + \sqrt{r^2 - d^2\sin^2 x}}{v}$$

Example:

Let us suppose that d = 150 m, z = 200, x = 30°, v = 300 m/s

So:

$$r^2 = 150^2 + 200^2 - 2 \times 150 \times 200\cos 30$$

$$r^2 = 17500$$

$$r = 132.3 \, m$$

$$TBVH = \frac{(150\cos 30) + \sqrt{132.3^2 - 150^2\sin^2 30}}{300}$$

$$TBVH = 0.7962 \, s$$
$$TBVH = 796.2 \, ms$$

3.1.2 Time Before Vertical Handover (for indoor environments) - Mobile node movement from a normal BS to BBS

This is the second case of the TBVH. It occurs when the MN moves under the coverage area of normal BS but towards the BBS with a velocity v as the following figure show:

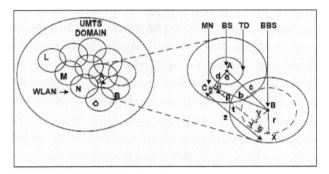

Fig (11): MN moves towards the BBS [29]

In the above figure, the concept of the threshold distance TD has been used in the normal BS. This distance is smaller than the radius of the cell which defines a small concentric circle that locates within the boundary of the cell. Since the MN moves inside the TD circle, it is more likely to change direction and vice versa. When the MN moves out of this circle, it has less change in direction which in turn makes it easier to make the correct prediction of the next cell that the MN moves towards. As the MN is far away from the BBS to get an accurate value of b, it is necessary therefore to find the distance and the angle β in order to get the ability to calculate z. Here, the same Pythagoras theorem will be applied taking into account the direction of the MN according to the following equation:

$$c^2 = d^2 + b^2 - 2db \cos \theta$$

When c is the point of the MN, d is the distance between the MN and the BS and b is the distance between the MN and the BBS.

$$\text{And, } \theta = \cos^{-1}\big((b^2 + d^2 - c^2)/2db\big)$$

33

$$\beta = |x - \theta|$$

Taking into consideration the triangle BYC so

$$t = b \cos \beta$$
$$y = b \sin \beta$$

Therefore, the value of s in the BYX triangle is

$$s = \sqrt{r^2 - b^2 \sin^2 \beta}$$

Since

$$z = t + s$$

So

$$z = b \cos \beta \sqrt{r^2 - b^2 \sin^2 \beta}$$

Since the velocity is the division of the distance over the time; therefore, TBVH for this case is:

$$TBVH = \frac{(b \cos \beta) + \sqrt{r^2 - d^2 \sin^2 \beta}}{v}$$

This is similar to the first equation of the previous case.

In the second case of TBVH it is easy to predicate accurately the TBVH due to the availability of the accurate topological information. Unlike the outdoor coverage, the calculation of TBVH does not only depend on the handover threshold due to the following reasons:

- When a mobile node moves under a small coverage such as WLAN, it is likely to expose frequent random movements and cause a frequent change in the direction. For example, when the mobile node moves towards the exit way, it might change in the direction and move in the opposite direction.
- When the mobile node appears, t moves closer to the threshold circle but in the direction of the wall instated of the direction of the exit as the following figure shows:

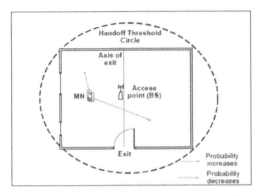

Fig (12): The mobile node in the indoor environment [30]

Finally, it is necessary to mention here that the value of TBVH alone is not enough to handoff, because the value of the MN reduces as the MN approaches the boundary of the coverage. But in reality, it cannot leave the WLAN coverage because it will be stopped by the wall. Therefore, to address this issue, a new mechanism has been suggested taking into account these random movements of the mobile node. This new mechanism can be summarized by assigning a W1which is the weight of the TBVH, and can be described as the cosine of the direction of the MN for a particular point of exit. So, as much as the value of W1 is high, it is likely to pass through the exit.

However, in multi exit point, the TBVH and the W1 will be calculated separately for each exit point. As a matter of fact, the TBVH mechanism for the indoor environments should have the ability to absorb the probability of having multiple exits points. In this case, TBVH and W1 should be calculated separately for each exits point whereas in the indoor case, the final probability in which the MN can be performed, a VHO is indicated by both TBVH and W1. However, when the MN moves out of the enclosed area, TBVH will be calculated as shown in the above equation of the outdoor environment.

Example:

Let us suppose that d = 100m, b = 200m, x = 30°, v = 400 m/s, r = 60m

So:

$c^2 = 100^2 + 200^2 - 2 \times 100 \times 200 \cos 30$

$c^2 = 15358.98$

$c = 123.93$

35

$$\theta = \cos^{-1}\left((200^2 + 100^2 - 123.93^2)/2 \times 100 \times 200\right)$$
$$\theta = \cos^{-1} 0.866$$
$$\theta = 29.999$$

$$\beta = |30 - 29.999|$$
$$\beta = 0.001$$

$$TBVH = \frac{(200 \cos 0.001) + \sqrt{60^2 - 100^2 \sin^2 0.001}}{400}$$

$$TBVH = 0.64999 \, s$$
$$TBVH = 649.99 \, m \, s$$

4. THE SIMULATION AND RESULT FOR THE TBVH

In this chapter, a program will be designed using Matlab software, flow charts will be designed and an investigation of the output results will be listed. However, it is necessary to explain why Matlab program specifically has been chosen.

4.1 Why Matlab program?

Matlab is the most suitable program for the mathematical calculations to get accurate results. According to Nguyen (2011) [19], Matlab software has several features which make it quite appropriate as the following points show:

- It performs mathematical calculation with speed and accurate results.

- It is easy and suitable for writing numerical programs.

- It has a high speed a good memory and easy to debug (run).

- It is very advance and has a performance debugger called a profile which has already built in the visualisation.

- It allows the user to access innumerable standards, equations and codes.

- It provides the user with a large variety of designing and modulating.

- It provides the user with the ability of showing figures, surfaces and simulink facility.

These features are the direct cause behind using Matlab as a simulation program to design and calculate TBVH.

4.2 Modulation

At the beginning of this section a block diagram for TBVH model has been designed with two input parameters: location coordination of the MN and location coordination of the BS as the following figure shows:

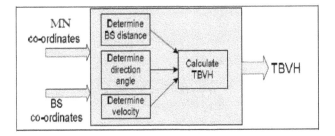

Fig (13): TBVH block diagram [30]

The above model has been designed to show the required parameters for calculating the TBVH. The question now is which of the two cases are going to be implemented to get an accurate result for the TBVH. According to the changes of the RSS for the CBS and the NXBS, the different cases of TBVH will be chosen. The following figure shows a flow chart which has been designed to solve this issue. Since, RSS of the next BS equals the RSS of the BBS, case two of TBVH will be chosen; otherwise it will be case one.

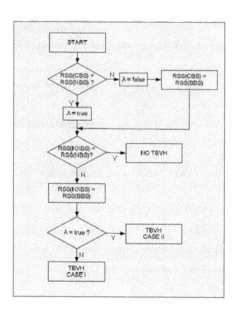

Fig (14): flow chart of TBVH choices [30]

Results of TBVH in matlab program will be listed in order to prove the manual calculations done earlier.

The following table shows TBVH for the first case (for the outdoor invirenment) by using Matlab program:

Table 3: calculating TBTH for the first case

Points	TBVH (seconds)
Point 1	8.3333
Point 2	6.3333
Point 3	4.6667
Point 4	3.3333
Point 5	2.3333
Point 6	1.0000
Point 7	0.6667

The following figure shows the relation between the distance and TBVH for the outdoor environment. It is a positive relationship which means that when the MN moves faraway from the BS, the value of TBVH will increase. For example, point 1 in table 3 shows the farthest distance for the MN from the BS and the TBVH is the longest time as well. On the other hand, point 7 is the closest distance to the BS and it has the shortest TBVH.

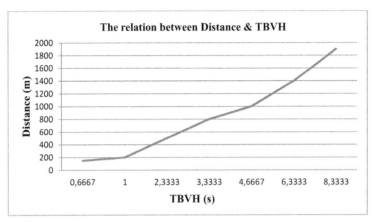

Fig (15): The relation between Distance & TBVH for the outdoor environment

Table 4: calculating TBVH for the first case before changing and after changing the direction. That happens when there is a change in the angle x and both of the distance d & z.

Points	TBVH before changing the direction (seconds)	TBVH after changing the direction (seconds)
Point 1	13.7500	30.000
Point 2	15.4450	46.3350
Point 3	24.9350	49.8700
Point 4	28.9300	57.8600
Point 5	43.8250	219.125
Point 6	49.3750	197.500
Point 7	55.4900	277.450

The above table shows that when the MN changes its direction (angle), the value of TBVH increases. Beacuse in this case the MN will move in the oposite direction or faraway from the BS which might consume more time to handoff.

The following table shows TBVH for the second case (for the indoor invirenment) by using Matlab program:

Table 5: calculating TBVH for the second case.

Points	TBVH (seconds)
Point 1	6.4000
Point 2	4.9000
Point 3	3.6500
Point 4	2.6500
Point 5	1.9000
Point 6	0.9000
Point 7	0.6500

Figure (16) shows the relation between the distance and TBVH for the indoor environment which has the same consept of the outdoor environment. The value of TBVH increases as long as the distance between the MN and the BBS increased. Point 7 in the above table shows the smallest distance which has the smallest value of TBVH unlike point 1 which has the largest distance with the largest value of the TBVH.

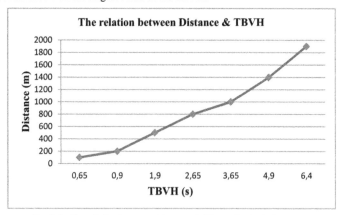

Fig (16): The relation between Distance & TBVH for the indoor envirenment

TBVH code in m-file by using matlab program in order to use this code for calculating different mobile nodes with different directions (angles) for the two cases of TBVH.

The pseudo code for the first case (Equation):

```
if (d > the allowable distance)
    z = (value of z);          %the distance when the MN expected to have VHO
    x = (angle of x);          % the angle made when MN moving towards the BBS
    v = (value of v)           %velocity of the MN;
    p = 2 * d * z * cos(x);
    o = (d^2) + (z^2) - p;
    r = sqrt (o);              % radius
    c = d * cos (x);
    h = o;
    m = (d^2);
    f = sin(x) ^2;
    s = h - (m * f);
    n = sqrt (s);
    TBVH = (c+n) / v;          % Time Before Vertical Handover
```

The pseudo code for the Second case (Equation):

```
elseif (the allowable distance > d > 0)
    b = 5;
    c = (value of c);          % the point of the MN
    x = (angle of x);
    v = (value of velocity);   %velocity of the MN;
    r = (value of radius);     % small value of radius
    m = (d^2);
    n = (b^2);
    g = 2 * d * b * cos (x);
    t = (n + m) - g;
    c = sqrt (t);
```

41

```
h = (n + m - t)/ (2 * d * b);
θ = acos (h);
B = x – θ;
y =  (sin (B)) ^2;
k = (r^2) – (m * y);
l = sqrt (k);
z = b * cos (B);
TBVH = (z+l) / v;          % Time Before Vertical Handover
```

The final case if the mobile node does not move and on the same point of the BS:

```
    else
    TBVH = 0;              % there will be no handover
end
```

If the mobile node remains on the same point of the BS i.e if the mobile does not move anywhere, there is no need to handoff the call and the signal will remain strong as it is. In this case the TBVH will be zero because there is no need to handoff the signall to other BSs or antennas.

4.3 Decision algorithm

In this part a pseudo code will be proposed in order to predicate the next position of the mobile node to handoff too and this algorithm is called decision algorithm for vertical handover and the following figure explains that:

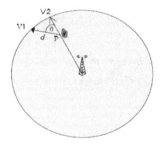

Fig (17): The decision algorithm for vertical handover [37]

42

While, P is the point when the MN makes a handover decision, V1 is the MN movement towards the point P; V2 is the direction from serving the BS to point P. θ is the angle between V1 and V2. d is the distance between point P to the border of the serving BS's coverage and in this case the coverage area has been taken as a circle instead of hexagon so d can be counted by the position of P and serving BS and coverage radius. Small v is the moving speed (magnitude) of the MN at point P. Alert RSS is a safe guard RSS which means there is no need to consider handover in this case. Margin is necessary for the existence of handover detecting interval and GSM positioning error, a certain handover advance margin must be near to the cell border in order to decrease the handover failure rate. When the outgoing time is taken into account, the margin can be used as the following (d – margin) / v is the outgoing time.

However, when the MN has a call or data stream below, handover detect should be executed continually. The detecting interval time might be adaptive to the speed of the MN in order to save power. When the MN moves faster, the needed interval time will be shorter. The following pseudo code shows the decision algorithm of this process:

```
Handoff Detect ()
{
if (A handover process is in progress and has not been finished)
Return;
if (RSS <= Alert RSS)
{
Update current speed and direction;
if (θ <= 90°)
{
  τ = estimate of handoff signalling delay;
  Go out time t = (d - margin)/v;
if (t <= τ)
{
  New BS = the nearest available neighbour BS from
          point P (available BSs means in the coverage of relative BSs);
  Handoff to new BS;
  }
 }
 }
}
```

43

The above pseudo cods can be used for several needs which might detect the Vertical handover decision, defined the distance and the time for vertical handover which can be done by knowing the speed of the MN.

5. Conclusion and Future

This paper has been divided into several parts with several subsections to cover the subject thoroughly. A clear definition of HO has been given with an explanation of its types and their differences. Also, the reasons behind failures in the HO technique have been adequately discussed as they often affect the signal of the GSM HO when the MN moves from one coverage area to another to avoid such obstacles. Moreover, the differences between the hard, soft and softer handovers and also between the SYNC and the asynchronous handovers have been shown too. In this paper, a new type of handover, the emergency handover, has been discussed as it can save and maintain the call. Furthermore, vertical and the horizontal handovers have been proposed even though the VHO has been given more attention. Also, brief descriptions about "Multilayer Handoff" Strategy, "Ping pong effect" and "take-back" have been given. HO decisions in GSM, issues facing the GSM HO and the solutions for these issues have been attentively observed in the last part of the literature review.

This project is based on Dr. Fatema Sabeen Shaikh's performed in 2010, especially when considering the velocity of the MN, the direction and the distance between the MN and the BS of VHO. Applying these entire parameters enable the researcher to calculate the TBVH in several points and cases. The differentiation between the two cases of calculating the TBVH has been based on Pythagoras theorem of the triangle, taking into account the direction and the location of the BS mobile node. The results of these equations have been proved manually using Matlab software to compare between the two results. Using Matlab can be a creative way for calculations because Matlab is the best program for doing the mathematical calculations of several equations and theories.

Further study might be carried on in the future to consider the threshold circle as a hexogen shape and the situation in the presence of three cells or more having several mobile nodes waiting to handoff simultaneously. The question is which one of them will have the priority and how is this going to affect the QoS of the process. Also, possible errors will be calculated; these errors might stem from the interference of other cells and whether the

44

calculating result will be different when using GPRS instead of the GSM. Moreover, for the security purposes, it is necessary to design and implement a complex model of calculating time and distance; therefore, the next step will be designing and implementing a program using C++ language with MySQL program. Using these two programs, the code of calculating time will be written using the C++ language and the data will be stored in the database of the MySQL program. This complex program will be the dawning of a new technique containing two different software in one program of accurate results and high security.

References

1. AKKi C.B & Chadchan S.M., "The Survey oh Handoff Issues in Wireless ATM Networks", 2008. [ONLINE] Available at: http://www.worldacademicunion.com/journal/1749-3889-3897IJNS/IJNSVol07No2Paper08.pdf. [Accessed 06 July 2011].

2. Bhatia A. & Stevetuf, "*Hard handoff*", Digital Communication - Wireless Technology 2008. [ONLINE] Available at: http://it.toolbox.com/wiki/index.php/Hard handoff. [Accessed 03 June 2011].

3. BING B., "Emerging Technologies in Wireless LANs" - Theory, Design and Deployment. Cambridge University Press, UK. 2008.

4. CAMPBELL, A.T. AND GOMEZ-CASTELLANOS, J. October. IP micro-mobility protocols. *ACM SIGMOBILE Mobile Computing and Communications Review* Vol. 4, Issue 4, 45-53, October 2000.

5. DUONG, H.H., DADEJ, A. AND GORDON, S. Proactive Context Transfer in WLAN-based Access Networks. *Proceedings of the 2nd ACM international workshop on Wireless mobile applications and services on WLAN hotspots*, 61-70. 2004.

6. Duval L., "GSM Call Management Procedures", 2006. [ONLINE] Available at: http://e-articles.info/e/a/title/GSM-Call-Management-Procedures/. [Accessed 04 June 2011].

7. EBERSMAN, H.G. AND TONGUZ, O.K. Handoff Ordering using Signal Prediction and Priority Queuing in Personal Communication Systems. *IEEE Transactions on Vehicular Technology* Vol. 48, 20-35. 1999.

8. EKiz N., "Modelling and analysis of multi-tier cellular networks with different queuing schemes", 2006. [ONLINE] Available at: http://www.belgeler.com/blg/19k0/modeling-and-analysis-of-multi-tier-cellular-networks-with-different-queuing-schemes-cok-katmanli-sebekelerin-cesitli-kuyruklama-tekniklerini-kullanarak-modellenmesi-ve-analizi. [Accessed 19 June 2011].

9. Ekiz N., Salih T., Kucukoner S. And Fidanboylu K., "An Overview of Hanoff Techniques in Cellular Networks" 2010. [ONLINE] Available at: http://www.google.co.uk/url?sa=t&source=web&cd=2&ved=0CCAQFjAB&url=http%3A%2F%2Fciteseerx.ist.psu.edu%2Fviewdoc%2Fdownload%3Fdoi%3D10.1.1.107.8649%26rep%3Drep1%26type%3Dpdf&rct=j&q=Ekiz%2C%20Salih%2C%20K%C3%BC%C3%A7%C3%BCk%C3%B6ner%20and%20Fidanboylu%20&ei=8vI9TrmdGYPqrQfS_pUQ&usg=AFQjCNE67AdSNebyvSYkYIhh8-GFqUSS9w&cad=rja. [Accessed 07 August 2011]. ETSI.Com, 2011. [ONLINE] Available at: http://www.etsi.org/WebSite/homepage.aspx. [Accessed 03 June 2011].

10. Freedman A., "Handoff in GSM/GPRS cellular system", 2011. [ONLINE] Available at: http://www.ieee802.org/21/archived_docs/Documents/OtherDocuments/Handoff_Fre edman.pdf. [Accessed 20 July 2011].

11. Ghini V.; Ferretti S.; Panzieri F; "A strategy for best access point selection", Dept. of Comput. Sci., Univ. of Bologna, Bologna, Italy, 2010. . [ONLINE] Available at: http://ieeexplore.ieee.org/xpl/freeabs_all.jsp?arnumber=5657762. [Accessed 21 July 2011].

12. 3Gmemories.Com, Google Image Result for http://3gmemories.com/files/2011/02/Hard-Handover.jpg. 2011. [ONLINE] Available at: http://www.google.co.uk/imgres?imgurl=http://3gmemories.com/files/2011/02/Hard -Handover.jpg&imgrefurl=http://3gmemories.com/tag/handover/&usg=_7a0Zr0-BlGdMf9rYMuuZffFlzW4=&h=180&w=490&sz=13&hl=en&start=64&zoom=1&tbnid=u HYm42XF0VcrBM:&tbnh=90&tbnw=276&ei=jzDpTYjHIYKAswbG1J2BCQ&prev=/searc h%3Fq%3Dhard%2Bhandover%26um%3D1%26hl%3Den%26sa%3DN%26biw%3D1 352%26bih%3D559%26tbm%3Disch&um=1&itbs=1&iact=hc&vpx=121&vpy=131&du r=31&hovh=136&hovw=371&tx=207&ty=87&page=4&ndsp=16&ved=1t:429,r:0,s:64& biw=1352&bih=559. [Accessed 03 June 2011].

13. Gnnettest.Com, "COMPASS Application Note 1 Handover Analysis", Denmark. 2011. [ONLINE] Available at: http://www.syrus.ru/files/solutions/control/nettest/compass/AN1_handover_analysis .pdf. [Accessed 02 June 2011].

14. ITU, "Considerations of horizontal handover and vertical handover", Mobile telecommunication networks, 2007. [ONLINE] Available at: http://www.itu.int/md/T05-SG19-C-0025/en. [Accessed 05 June 2011].

15. Khan R., "Soft and Softer Handover in WCDMA", 2010. [ONLINE] Available at: http://www.scribd.com/doc/46265448/Soft-and-Softer-Handover-in-WCDMA. [Accessed 03 June 2011].

16. Latif M. & Khan A., "QUALITY OF SERVICE DURING VERTICAL HANDOVER IN 3G/4G WIRELESS NETWORKS",Table 4.1: Difference between Vertical/Horizontal Handover. 2009. [ONLINE] Available at: http://www.scribd.com/doc/39159214/94/Table-4-1-Difference-between-Vertical-Horizontal-Handover. [Accessed 04 June 2011].

17. MING-HSING CHIU AND BASSIOUNI, M.A. Predictive schemes for handoff prioritization in cellular networks based on mobile positioning. *IEEE Journal on Selected Areas in Communications* Vol. 18, Issue 3. 510-522. 2000.

18. Nguyen T., "Matlab Simulink" 2011. [ONLINE] Available at: http://www.google.co.uk/url?sa=t&source=web&cd=2&sqi=2&ved=0CCEQFjAB&url=ht tp%3A%2F%2Fpersonal.rhul.ac.uk%2Fusah%2F080%2FQITNotes_files%2FMatlabIntr o.doc&rct=j&q=why%20matlab%20for%20calculation%20instead%20of%20other%20 programs&ei=5D4qTpjeFYborQfx94myDQ&usg=AFQjCNGjunwxm38e0NrRPANZaEInM Culkw&cad=rja. [Accessed 23 July 2011].

19. Dr. Pesch D.H, "GSM Concepts", 2000. [ONLINE] Available at: http://www.scribd.com/doc/55086776/1/GSM-Concepts. [Accessed 08 July 2011]. 22

20. Phonehistory.co.uk, "Mobile Phones - How it works – Handoffs" - The history of mobile phones!. 2011. [ONLINE] Available at: http://www.phonehistory.co.uk/mobile-phone-how-it-works-handoffs.html. [Accessed 20 July 2011].

21. Pram. Web, "Handoff in CDMA (Types, Mechanism, and It's Parameters)", 2008. [ONLINE] Available at: http://pram.web.id/blog/2008/05/16/handoff-in-cdma-types-mechanism-and-its-parameters/. [Accessed 04 June 2011].

22. Protocols.Com, "Telephony Protocols | Including GSM Standard - BSSAP | BSSMAP | GSM L3 | RR | MM | CC | SMS | Mobile IP", 2011.. [ONLINE] Available at: http://www.protocols.com/pbook/telephony.htm. [Accessed 03 June 2011].

23. Radio-Electronics.Com, "GSM Handover or Handoff [11]", 2011. [ONLINE] Available at: http://www.radio-electronics.com/info/cellulartelecomms/gsm_technical/handover-handoff.php. [Accessed 02 June 2011].

24. Radio-Electronics.Com, "GSM History [2]", 2011. [ONLINE] Available at: http://www.radio-electronics.com/info/cellulartelecomms/gsm_technical/gsm-history.php. [Accessed 19 July 2011].

25. Rajkamalvashistha, "Synchronous and asynchronous handover" - GSM for Dummies, 2011. [ONLINE] Available at: http://www.gsmfordummies.com/forum/discussion/2/synchronous-and-asynchronous-handover/p1. [Accessed 04 June 2011].

26. Ramsdal, P. A. And Harrold, W. B., "Techniques for Cellular Networks Incorporating Microcells", Proceeding of Personal, Indoor and Mobile Radio Communications (PIMRC'92), 1992.

27. Ramsdale P., Walden, Gaskell P., "Handover techniques" - Google Patents. 1994. [ONLINE] Available at: http://www.google.co.uk/patents?hl=en&lr=&vid=USPAT5278991&id=ZnEjAAAAEBAJ &oi=fnd&dq=Handover+techniques++Peter+A.+Ramsdale+et+al&printsec=abstract#v= onepage&q=Handover%20techniques%20%20Peter%20A.%20Ramsdale%20et%20al &f=false. [Accessed 02 June 2011].

28. Shaikh F., (2010), "Intelligent Proactive Handover and QoS Management using TBVH in Heterogeneous Network", Middlesex University, London.

29. Shaikh F., Lasebae A., and Glenford Mapp, "Proactive Policy Management for Heterogeneous Networks" 2010. [ONLINE] Available at: http://www.mdx.ac.uk/Assets/ICTTA_08%283%29.pdf. [Accessed 14 July 2011].

30. SHEN, X., MARK, J.W. AND YE, J. User Mobility Profile Prediction: An Adaptive Fuzzy Inference Approach. *Wireless Networks* Vol. 6, 363-374, 2000.

31. STUBER, G.L. Principles of Mobile Communication. Second Edition, Kluwer Academic Publishers, Norwell, MA. 2001.

32. Thomsen J. & Manggaard R. "Analysis of GSM Handover using Coloured Petri Nets- GSM Handover Failure", 2003. [ONLINE] Available at: http://www.scribd.com/doc/59105598/Gsm-HandOver-Failure. [Accessed 09 July 2011].

33. Umair M., "What are emergency handovers?", 2009. [ONLINE] Available at: http://www.allinterview.com/showanswers/81892.html. [Accessed 05 June 2011].

34. UMTS.Com, "*UMTS handover*", 2011. [ONLINE] Available at: http://www.umtsworld.com/technology/handover.htm. [Accessed 03 June 2011].

35. UMTS Tutorial.Com, "Handover principle and concepts". 2011. [ONLINE] Available at: http://www.3g4g.co.uk/Tutorial/ZG/zg_handover.html. [Accessed 02 June 2011].

36. Wang F., IEEE Explore –"Position Aware Vertical Handoff Decision Algorithm in Heterogeneous Wireless Networks", 2011. [ONLINE] Available at: http://ieeexplore.ieee.org/xpl/freeabs_all.jsp?arnumber=4677940. [Accessed 03 August 2011].

37. Wowra J., "Handover in DVB-H" 2011. [ONLINE] Available at: http://user.informatik.uni-goettingen.de/~seminar/dvb/DVBHandover_JWowra.pdf. [Accessed 19 June 2011].

38. XIAOHUAN YAN, MANI, N. AND CEKERCIOGLU, Y.A. A Travelling Distance Prediction Based Method to Minimize Unnecessary Handovers from Cellular Networks to WLANs. *IEEE Communications Letters* Vol. 12, 14-16. 2008a.

39. XIAOHUAN YAN, SEKERCIOGLU, Y.A. AND MANI, N. A method for minimizing unnecessary handovers in heterogeneous wireless networks. *Proceedings of International Symposium on World of Wireless, Mobile and Multimedia Networks,* 1-5. 2008b.

Yan X., 2010, "Optimization of Vertical Handover Decision Processes for Fourth Generation Heterogeneous Wireless Networks". [ONLINE] Available at: http://titania.ctie.monash.edu.au/pgrad-projects/iris_vhd.pdf. [Accessed 13 July 2011].

www.ingramcontent.com/pod-product-compliance
Lightning Source LLC
La Vergne TN
LVHW042258060326
832902LV00009B/1120